# Ancient Greece

**SANDRA NEWMAN**

**Children's Press®**
An Imprint of Scholastic Inc.
New York  Toronto  London  Auckland  Sydney
Mexico City  New Delhi  Hong Kong
Danbury, Connecticut

**Content Consultant**
Dimitri Nakassis
Assistant Professor
Department of Classics
University of Toronto


Library of Congress Cataloging-in-Publication Data

Newman, Sandra, 1965-
    Ancient Greece / by Sandra Newman.
        p. cm.—(A true book)
    Includes index.
        ISBN-13: 978-0-531-25226-0 (lib. bdg.)        978-0-531-24107-3 (pbk.)
        ISBN-10: 0-531-25226-4 (lib. bdg.)        0-531-24107-6 (pbk.)

1. Greece—Civilization—To 146 B.C.—Juvenile literature.  I. Title. II. Series.

DF77.N47 2009
938—dc22                            2008052548

1 2 3 4 5 6 7 8 9 10 R 19 18 17 16 15 14 13 12 11 10                    62

# Find the Truth!

**Everything** you are about to read is true *except* for one of the sentences on this page.

Which one is **TRUE**?

**T or F**   Everyone could vote in ancient Greece.

**T or F**   The Olympic Games began as a festival to honor ancient gods.

Find the answers in this book.

# Contents

**The Greek god, Poseidon (poh-SYE-don)**

The ancient Greeks gave laurel wreaths to winners of Olympic events. ➡

## THE BIG TRUTH!

## The First Olympics

What kinds of sports did people play in ancient Greece? . . . . . . . . . . . . . . . . . . . . . . . . . **26**

## 5 Arts and Sciences

What kind of entertainment did the ancient Greeks like? . . . . . . . . . . . . . . . . . . . . **31**

## 6 From Greece to Rome

Who conquered ancient Greece? . . . . . . . . . . . . **37**

The Erechtheum
(i-REK-thee-uhm) is
an ancient Greek temple
that is famous for its
detailed columns.

# CHAPTER 1

# Greek Glories

The ancient Greeks may have lived thousands of years ago, but their ideas are still part of our lives today. Many important ideas about laws and government came from the ancient Greeks. Subjects that you learn about in school, like math and science, also got their start in ancient Greece. Even the design of the buildings around you may have come from the ancient Greeks.

The ancient Greeks were famous for using columns in their buildings.

# New Ideas, New Worlds

Ancient Greece was a very important **civilization** (si-ve-li-ZAY-shen) of the ancient world. Many of today's ideas and customs had their roots in ancient Greece. The ancient Greeks created works of art and poetry, made scientific discoveries, and shaped ways of thought, that are still studied today.

Greek-style columns can be seen in buildings all over the world.

The Temple of Olympian Zeus in Athens, Greece.

But we've learned more than science and art from ancient Greece. The ancient Greeks inspired the people who came after them to view the world in a whole new way. Earlier civilizations thought that following old traditions was important.

They didn't like new ideas. The ancient Greeks were some of the first people to believe that new ideas could make life better for everyone.

**The United States Capitol building**

Macedonia

Troy

Aegean Sea

Ionian Sea

(Present-day
TURKEY)

Corinth

Athens

Peloponnesus

Sparta

Cythera

Antikythera

Mediterranean Sea

Crete

Ancient Greece

# CHAPTER 2

# The Birth of Ancient Greece

Ancient Greece was located in what is now southern Europe, on the Balkan **Peninsula** (pe-NIN-se-le). It also included hundreds of small islands in the Aegean Sea. Areas of modern-day Turkey were once part of ancient Greece as well.

Ancient Greece is often called the "cradle of Western civilization."

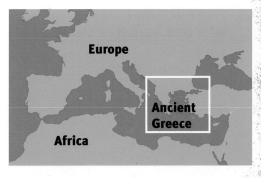

# The Early Greeks

Two of the earliest known civilizations in ancient Greece were the Minoans (min-NOH-ans) and the Mycenaeans (my-si-NEE-uns). The Minoans built palaces on the island of Crete in 1900 B.C.E. Beginning in 1400 B.C.E., the Mycenaeans built palaces on the Greek mainland. Both the Minoans and the Mycenaeans were great shipbuilders and traded goods with other countries. They also created beautiful cloth and pottery.

**This is the golden death mask of a Mycenaean ruler who was buried in about 1600 B.C.E.**

# The Trojan War

According to Greek legend, the Trojan War began when a prince from the city of Troy kidnapped a Greek queen named Helen. The Greeks hid soldiers inside a huge wooden horse to sneak into Troy. **Historians** thought that the war was just a story until 1870. That's when the ruins of a city that could have been Troy were discovered in the country of Turkey.

It is still not known for sure whether the Trojan War really happened. But if it did, it probably occurred during the time of the Mycenaeans.

**The Trojan horse**

# The Greek Dark Ages

**The Lion Gate, which dates back to the ancient city of Mycenae, still stands today.**

In about 1200 B.C.E., the Mycenaean palaces were burned to the ground. Experts are not sure why this happened. After this most people became very poor. They stopped writing and didn't create as much art, so not many records of this time exist. Also at this time, trade between the people of ancient Greece and other parts of Europe and Asia may have slowed down. Since not much is known about this period, historians call this time the "Greek Dark Ages."

# A Rise to Power

About 700 B.C.E., life began to change in ancient Greece. Greek cities started forming their own governments. Ancient Greeks began to study science, art, theater, and poetry. A Greek alphabet was created. All of these exciting new ideas would someday make ancient Greece one of the most admired civilizations of the ancient world.

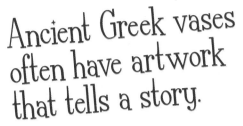
Ancient Greek vases often have artwork that tells a story.

This is what a Greek city-state may have looked like.

# CHAPTER 3

# The Growth of Government

Ancient Greece was never a country with one government. Instead, it contained many **city-states**. A city-state was made up of one city and the small villages around it. Each city-state had its own government and laws. Since they were all ruled differently, ancient Greek city-states used many different systems of government.

*Polis was the Greek word for city-state.*

**Sparta was one of the few city-states that had kings who handed their thrones down to their children.**

## Types of Governments

Some city-states had one ruler who, like a king, was not chosen by the people. This kind of government was a **tyranny** (TE-re-ne). City-states ruled by a few people were called **oligarchies** (O-li-gar-kees). Some cities were **democracies** (di-MO-kre-sees). Democracies allow their citizens to choose leaders in their government.

## Sparta, Land of Soldiers

One of the most famous city-states in ancient Greece was Sparta. This city-state became powerful during the 7th century B.C.E. Sparta's success was mainly due to the fact that Spartan men were the finest warriors in all of ancient Greece. These men grew up learning how to fight. They were taken from their homes at the age of seven to join the military.

Sparta was the only city-state that educated girls.

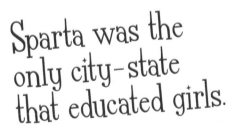

# Athens, Home of Democracy

Athens was a city-state that became powerful during the 5th century B.C.E. It was known for its great artists, poets, and thinkers. Most of the ancient Greek writings we still read today are from Athens. The government in Athens was a democracy that was divided into two main groups—the Boule (BOO-lee) and the Assembly. Members of the Boule were chosen by chance from a group of citizens. But any citizen could be a member of the Assembly.

20

For important votes, at least 6,000 members had to attend the Assembly.

**Women and slaves did not have the same rights as men in ancient Greece.**

# Not for Everyone

Even in democracies like Athens, not everyone had a say in the government. To vote, you had to be an adult man. Women did not get to vote. Neither did **immigrants** (IM-uh-gruhnts), who were people that came to ancient Greece from other places. Many people in ancient Greece were slaves. Slaves had none of the rights of citizens. People often became slaves when their city was conquered by another city.

Ancient Greek temples, like the Parthenon (PAR-the-non), were covered with sculptures of gods, heroes, and monsters.

# CHAPTER 4

# The Gods of Greece

Religion was very important to the ancient Greeks. They believed in many gods that looked and acted like humans. But unlike humans, the gods were very powerful and lived forever. The ancient Greeks believed that the gods played a part in everything that happened on Earth. The gods were even written about in stories called **myths** (MITHS).

The Parthenon was a temple built to honor the goddess Athena (uh-THEE-nuh).

**Goddess Athena**

# Many Gods

Each god or goddess ruled over a few special areas. For example, Apollo (uh-PALL-loh) was the god of music, poetry, and archery. His sister Artemis (ARE-tih-muhss) was the goddess of hunting.

The gods also had a king called Zeus (ZOOSE), who ruled over them. According to Greek myths, the gods lived on Mount Olympus (uh-LIM-pus), which was the tallest mountain in ancient Greece.

# Guide to Gods and Goddesses

1. **Aphrodite (AF-froh-DYE-tee):** Goddess of love and beauty

2. **Ares (AIR-eez):** God of war and bloodshed

3. **Hermes (HER-meez):** Messenger of the gods

4. **Hestia (HES-tee-uh):** Goddess of the home and cooking

5. **Poseidon (poh-SYE-don):** God of the sea, earthquakes, and horses

6. **Athena (uh-THEE-nuh):** Goddess of wisdom and warfare

7. **Zeus (ZOOSE):** Ruler of the gods and the god of sky, thunder, and lightning

8. **Hera (HAIR-uh):** The wife of Zeus and the goddess of women, marriage, and childbirth

9. **Apollo (uh-PALL-loh):** God of music, poetry, and archery

10. **Artemis (ARE-tih-muhss):** Goddess of hunting, wilderness, and young girls

11. **Hephaestus (heh-FIGH-stus):** God of fire and metalworkers

12. **Demeter (da-MEE-ta):** Goddess of agriculture

Greek sports included wrestling, foot races, boxing, and racing carts called chariots.

# The First Olympics

For the Greeks, sports had a religious meaning. When important leaders died, sports matches were held. Ancient Greek competitions also celebrated the gods. The Olympic Games honored the ruler of all Greek gods, Zeus. They were first held in the valley of Olympia in 776 B.C.E.

The ancient Greeks believed that sports helped prepare men for battle.

## Like Humans

In ancient Greek myths, the gods sometimes misbehaved and played tricks on humans. One of the most famous ancient Greek myths was about the sailor, Odysseus (oh-DIH-see-us). In this story, the gods forced Odysseus to wander the ocean for ten long years.

**The Odyssey** is the well-known story of Odysseus' journey.

# Worshipping the Gods

The ancient Greeks had many temples and each was dedicated to a different god. On altars located outside of these temples, ancient Greeks would **sacrifice** (SA-kre-fize) or give up their prized animals to the gods. They hoped these sacrifices would make the gods happy and that the gods would help them in return.

This carving shows a sacrifice being made to the gods.

Greeks also left small carvings or statues in temples as sacrifices.

Euclid

# CHAPTER 5

# Arts and Sciences

The ancient Greeks were famous for their new ideas in art, poetry, math, and science. Greek thinkers like Euclid (YOO-klid) and Pythagoras (pih-THAH-gor-ruhs) invented geometry, the mathematical study of shapes. Greek writers such as Sophocles (SO-fe-kleez) and Euripides (ye-RI-pe-deez) wrote plays that people still enjoy today.

For more than 2,000 years people have been reading Euclid's book *Elements,* which is about math.

# Poetry

During early times in ancient Greece, musicians were like poets that traveled from city to city. They would sing their poems and play stringed instruments called lyres (LYERS). Most poems were stories about heroes and the gods. Later, popular poems were written down. Some were very short, like modern songs. But other early poems were hundreds of pages long!

This painting from a Greek vase shows musicians playing a harp, lyre, and cithara (kee-TA-ra), the ancient version of the guitar.

Actors in ancient Greece performed in masks that covered their faces.

## Theater

The ancient Greeks created the art of theater. Every year in Athens, there was a festival dedicated to Dionysus (die-oh-NIE-sus), the god of wine and theater. Everyone in the city gathered to watch plays for three whole days. Plays were performed on outdoor stages. People in the audience sat on steps that surrounded the stage.

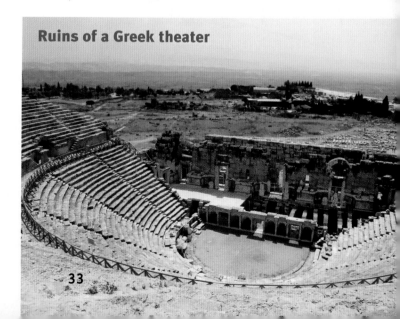

Ruins of a Greek theater

33

# Found at Sea

In 1901, a group of divers found an ancient shipwreck off the Greek island of Antikythera (an-ti-ki-THEER-uh). The wreck was full of beautiful statues made of bronze and marble. The divers also found a strange tool. It had thirty bronze gears and a crank. Divers named the tool the Antikythera mechanism (ME-ke-ni-zem). Ancient Greeks used this tool to estimate the position of the Sun, Moon, and planets on certain dates.

**The Antikythera mechanism**

# Great Thinkers

Socrates (SOC-kre-teez) was one of the greatest thinkers of ancient Greece. He lived in the 5th century B.C.E. Socrates asked his students questions because he wanted them to think for themselves. Many other ancient Greek thinkers were influenced by the teachings of Socrates.

**Statue of Socrates**

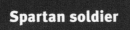

Spartan soldier

# CHAPTER 6

# From Greece to Rome

After the 6th century B.C.E., things began to change again in ancient Greece. Cities were being attacked by the Persian Empire in the east. After a long war between Athens and Sparta, ancient Greece was no longer as powerful as it had once been.

Boys in Sparta began training to be warriors at the age of seven.

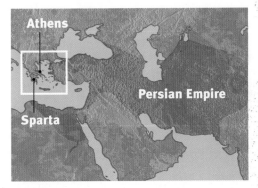

Athens

Sparta

Persian Empire

# The Peloponnesian War

For many years, Athens and Sparta were the most powerful city-states in ancient Greece. But these two city-states had very different cultures and didn't always agree. In 431 B.C.E, a series of battles called the Peloponnesian (pel-e-pe-NEE-shun) War finally broke out between Athens and Sparta. It lasted for 27 years and left ancient Greece in ruins.

**Greek soldiers were called hoplites (HOP-lites). They were heavily armed with helmets, shields, and spears.**

# Alexander the Great

The Peloponnesian War wasn't the end of ancient Greece. Under King Alexander the Great, ancient Greece rose one more time. Alexander's father, Philip II, had ruled over all of the city-states and built a powerful army. After his father died, Alexander led Greek armies to conquer Persia, Egypt, and parts of India.

**This is a piece of a mosaic showing Alexander the Great in battle. A mosaic is a picture made with small tiles.**

Alexander the Great was only 20 years old when he became king.

## After Alexander

When Alexander the Great died in 323 B.C.E., his empire was split into three main states. This marked the beginning of the Hellenistic (he-le-NI-stik) Period. Hellenistic empires were ruled by kings who paid for great libraries and palaces. This was an important time of learning for scholars and scientists in ancient Greece. But it did not last forever.

## Ancient Greece Timeline

**1600** ➡ **776**
**B.C.E.** **B.C.E.**

**Mycenaean** **First Olympic Games**
**civilization**
**begins.**

# Hellenistic Empires

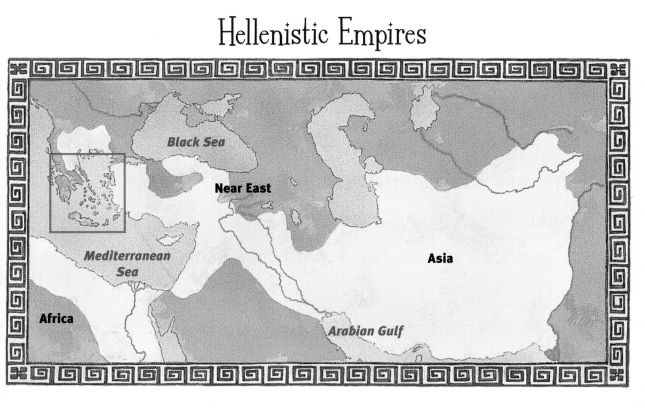

Black Sea

Near East

Mediterranean Sea

Asia

Africa

Arabian Gulf

**KEY**

Hellenistic Empires     Ancient Greece

## 146 B.C.E.
**Greece becomes part of the Roman Empire.**

## 336 B.C.E.
**Alexander the Great becomes king.**

Colosseum in Rome

# The Rise of Rome

As the years passed, Greece slowly grew weaker. But the neighboring Roman Empire, in Italy, was growing stronger. In 146 B.C.E., Greece finally became part of the Roman Empire. The ancient Romans respected the ancient Greeks' many accomplishments. The Romans even continued to use the Greek language in their writings. Through the ancient Romans, the ideas of the ancient Greeks continued to shape peoples' lives and are still known to us today. ★

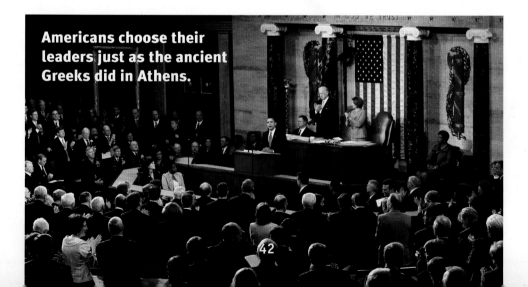

**Americans choose their leaders just as the ancient Greeks did in Athens.**

# True Statistics

**Number of ancient Greek city-states:** More than 1,500

**Number of Greek gods:** Hundreds

**Year of the first Olympic Games:** 776 B.C.E.

**Number of people in ancient Athens:** About 250,000—the same as Boise, Idaho

**Number of people who could vote in Athens:** About 30,000

**Height of Mount Olympus:** 9,570 ft. (2,917 m)

**Year of birth of Alexander the Great:** 356 B.C.E.

## Did you find the truth?

**(F)** Everyone could vote in ancient Greece.

**(T)** The Olympic Games began as a festival to honor ancient gods.

# Resources

## Books

Augustin, Byron, and Rebecca A. Augustin, *Greece* (A to Z). New York: Children's Press, 2005.

Chisholm, Jane, Lisa Miles, and Struan Reid. *Encyclopedia of Ancient Greece*. London, United Kingdom: Usborne Books, 2007.

Connolly, Peter. *The Ancient Greece of Odysseus*. Oxford, UK: Oxford University Press, 1998.

Cooney, Caroline B. *Goddess of Yesterday*. New York: Delacourt Press, 2002.

Gay, Kathlyn. *Science in Ancient Greece*. New York: Franklin Watts, 1998.

Lassieur, Allison. *The Ancient Greeks* (People of the Ancient World). New York: Franklin Watts, 2004.

Pearson, Anne. *Ancient Greece* (Eyewitness). New York: DK Pub., 2007.

Whiting, Jim. *The Life and Times of Aristotle*. Hockessin, DE: Mitchell Lane Publishers, 2007.

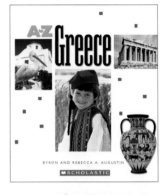

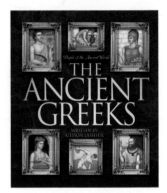

# Organizations and Web Sites

## Social Studies for Kids: Ancient Greece

www.socialstudiesforkids.com/subjects/ancientgreece.htm
Check out the Ancient Greece Glossary to learn more about
famous people and places.

## Ancient Greece for Kids

www.greece.mrdonn.org
Learn more about the history and everyday life of the ancient
Greeks and play games.

## BBC Schools: Ancient Greece

www.bbc.co.uk/schools/ancientgreece
Click on Cartoon Classics to read an online comic book about
the ancient Olympic Games.

# Places to Visit

## The Metropolitan Museum of Art

1000 Fifth Avenue
New York, NY 10028
(212) 535 7710
www.metmuseum.org
The Greek and Roman galleries contain thousands of objects from the ancient Greek world.

## The Parthenon in Nashville

Centennial Park
2600 West End Avenue
Nashville, TN 37203
(615) 862 8431
www.nashville.gov/parthenon
Visit a reconstruction of the Parthenon, a temple for the goddess Athena, as it was in the golden age of Athens.

# Important Words

**city-states** – cities and the villages around them that had their own independent government

**civilization** (si-ve-li-ZAY-shen) – the way of life of a people

**democracies** (di-MO-kre-sees) – type of governments where citizens elect their leaders

**historians** – people that study history

**immigrants** (IM-uh-gruhnts) – people who live permanently in countries where they weren't born

**myths** (MITHS) – stories about the shared beliefs of a group of people, often about gods or goddesses

**oligarchies** (O-li-gar-kees) – governments that are ruled by a few people

**peninsula** (pe-NIN-se-le) – a narrow strip of land nearly surrounded by water

**sacrifice** (SA-kre-fize) – to offer a gift to a honor a god

**tyranny** (TE-re-ne) – a government in which all power is in the hands of a single ruler

# Index

Page numbers in **bold** indicate illustrations

# About the Author

Sandra Newman is the author of the award-nominated *The Only Good Thing Anyone Has Ever Done* (HarperCollins) and *Cake* (Random House). She co-authored the writing manual *How Not to Write a Novel* with Howard Mittelmark, which was published in 2008. For children, she is also the author of *A True Book: Europe*. Ms. Newman has taught at Temple University, the University of Colorado, and Chapman University. She lives in New York City.